To :-

From :-

'TO A VERY SPECIAL'® AND 'TO-GIVE-AND-TO-KEEP'® ARE
REGISTERED TRADE MARKS OF EXLEY PUBLICATIONS LTD AND
EXLEY GIFTBOOKS.

Other mini books in the series:

To a very Special Daughter   To a very Special Friend
To a very Special Granddaughter To a very Special Grandmother
To a very Special Grandpa   Happy Anniversary
Happy Retirement   To my very Special Husband
To my very Special Love   To a very Special Mother
To a very Special Sister   To a very Special Son
To my very Special Wife   Wishing you Happiness

Dedicated to my own special Dad – with lots of love from Juliette

Published simultaneously in 1993 by Exley Giftbooks in the USA and
Exley Publications Ltd in Great Britain.

24   23   22   21   20   19   18   17   16   15   14

Illustrations copyright © Helen Exley 1993
Selection copyright © Helen Exley 1993
The moral right of the author has been asserted.

ISBN 1-85015-396-5 (Laminate edition)
     1-86187-028-0 (Personalised suedel edition)
     1-86187-063-9 (Suedel edition)

A copy of the CIP data is available from the British Library on request.

Edited by Helen Exley.
Illustrations by Juliette Clarke.
Written by Pam Brown.
Typesetting by Delta, Watford
Printed in Hungary.

Exley Publications Ltd, 16 Chalk Hill, Watford, Herts WD1 4BN,
United Kingdom
Exley Publications LLC, 232 Madison Avenue, Suite 1206,
NY 10016, USA.

To a very special
DAD

Written by Pam Brown
Illustrations by Juliette Clarke

Thank you not so much for what
you taught me or gave me – but just
for being you.

. . .

A HELEN EXLEY GIFTBOOK

EXLEY
NEW YORK • WATFORD, UK

A FATHER IS...

... an ordinary man doing his best to stand in for
Superman.

... a source of good but usually expendable advice.

... a very-nearly expert.

... a man who knows - but would like to look it up
just to be on the safe side.

... a man who goes down fighting.

. . .

Dads are most ordinary men turned by love into adventurers, story-tellers, singers of songs.

Dads can do anything. The youth of dads was packed with excitement and their minds are packed with anecdotes. They have sound views on politics, dogs, sport and saving the environment. They have drawers and boxes and sheds full of valuable gadgets. And string. They can tell unforgettable stories.

There really *is* a touch of magic in a dad. They are no longer ordinary men. They are special.

. . .

You know a man is an established father when you see him carrying a potty through a parking lot.

. . .

Dads know more about things than you'd credit. Only it's best to check before you hand it in as homework.

. . .

HOME

The best sound of childhood
was your key in the door.

. . .

I used to sit in your chair till
you came home. It was the
special place to wait, the
place that held the shape
of you, the smell of your
books, the old cushion you
tucked into your back.
We threw out the chair.
But I still miss it when
you're not around.

. . .

Do you remember, Dad, those days when all my world was home? How little things loomed large? I did not know your wider universe - but you bent down and shared my rainbow puddles, frog faces peering from the pool, the iridescence of a beetle's wing, pebbles and bottle tops. All equal magic. You showed me secret things - hyacinths nosing through the earth in spring. A nut rasped open by a bird's beak. Seeds sprouting. Tracks of a dog's paw padded in the dust.

You lifted me high on your shoulders and let me touch the trees. You gave me a shell to keep.

I think perhaps I gave you something too - a world you'd half forgotten.

And a small hand in yours.

I've grown since then - but that long friendship has outlasted all change.

And all you gave me is a part of me forever.

. . .

ALWAYS MY PROTECTOR

A wise dad knows a quiet hug heals most hurts.

. . .

High on your shoulders under the singing trees, my hands held tight in yours - or striding over hills at a giant's height, the world below me. And safe - sure that I would not fall.

Tired at the day's end, your arms about me, my face against your shoulder. Smell of your jacket under my nose and jogging gently home. Or snuggled beneath your coat at a bus stop, tented against the rain and gathering dark - drowsing against you as the night slipped by. Safe. Sure. Heading home.

. . .

 Thank you for shrinking to my size when we played and expanding to great heights when I needed shelter and protection.

Fear, and threatening shadows on the wall. The room grown unfamiliar. The bedclothes tangled. A yellow square of light. Gentle and sure your arms about me, lifting me free - setting me safe in the chair until the furrows and heat have been smoothed away. All safe. All cool and soft and welcoming. A sip of water. The beginnings of a story whose end is lost in sleep.

And you there - and so ... all safe.

My shield from all harm.

Giving me certainty - that safe, still place to which I can always turn.

. . .

TO ALL THE ORDINARY DADS!

Children love their fathers down to the very last detail. The little patch balding on the top of his head. The set of his eyebrows. The shape of his ears. The small split that torments his thumb in winter. The silver scar across his knuckles. The scent of glue or soap or garden earth. Each of these learned by heart and stored away.

Everyone knows Dad's jokes by heart. That's why they are special.

. . .

Dads make stupendous, colossal, gigantic, enormous mistakes.

They've been doing it for millions of years. And don't worry, Dad ... lots of it was our fault anyway!

. . .

I give you a toast. To all the dads who've had their lives turned upside down by The State of the Economy. Who in one swoop have lost prestige, routine, income and mates. And yet survive – and make a brand new life. Who discover new abilities. Who use the extra time to build, from what would be ruin, a richer, happier life for their kids... and for their wives. And for themselves.

To all the dads learning new jobs, honing old skills, digging ponds, building pergolas, fixing the roof, taking the kids to playschool, baking fruit cakes, running classes, doing degrees.

Beginning all over again.

. . .

MEMORIES OF HAPPY DAYS

We may have been rich or we may have been poor
when I was young.

All I know was that we *felt* rich. For there was
always love and there were always surprises.

. . .

I never forget Dad Bathnights.

We always flooded the floor.

Well, you *do* when there are whales in
the bath - or you're demonstrating waterskiing
with a loofah.

. . .

Thanks for all the good memories, Dad. The time we cooked a surprise supper ... an amazingly surprising supper. The time we went for a walk in the rain ... and everyone stared at us from their windows. The time we went for a train trip ... just for the ride there and back. The time we dug the pond ...

in the wrong place.

All the happy times, Dad.

. . .

Do you remember Dad Cooking Days? Your mother's recipes. Treacle and spices. Butter and flour. Fruit and sugar. Fragrance and spillages. Mother shut out. Mountains of dirty dishes. And family meals I'll never forget.

. . .

In memories of childhood you are beside me, listening, explaining, cuddling me...
You will always be a part of me, Dad.

. . .

THE DEFENDER

Fathers as far as possible avoid fights and trouble, avoid confrontation. Put out the garbage quietly and tidily. Keep down the weeds. Stand waiting without argument. Are courteous to teachers.

But see them when their children are at risk - or wrongly accused - or injured. Not even Superman is so dramatically transformed. Relatives and park keepers and schoolteachers shrivel before them. They swoop down and rescue their threatened children.

. . .

Thank you, Dad, for making me feel important - to you and to the world. Thank you for helping me believe I can do something well. Thank you for changing other people's "You obviously can't do it" to "You obviously can't do it. Yet ... Let's take another look."

Thank you for walking the path beside me - pointing out the potholes and the slippery patches. Thank you for recognizing the moment when I could work things out for myself - and letting me go on alone. But never completely alone. Knowing you were there - at the end of a phone. At a place where I could always find you.

. . .

We looked to you for justice and advice in everything from the internal combustion engine to baking cakes - and we got it. And announced with confidence, "My Dad says ... ".

. . .

YOUR HANDS

I would watch your expert hands when I was
small. Working on an engine. Fixing shelves.
Sewing my teddy bear. Digging. Now as
I work I feel your presence. My own hands
echo yours.

. . .

You held my hands when I was afraid, when I was
ill, when I was weary, when I was bewildered.
Hoisted on your shoulders I saw the world.
I saw the world, anchored by your steady grip. I
watched your hands work. I wondered at their skill.
You let me venture. You let me go.
But touched my shoulder when I needed comfort
and assurance.
And if those hands have changed with the passing
years, they are still my father's hands -
that touch me with love.

. . .

OUR HERO

You were so strong, so tall, so wise. You were the mender of broken things, supplier of needs, giver of rewards. You were the source of all the best stories, the singer of songs, the deviser of games. You held all facts and figures in your head, knew all the rules, all laws. You were the dispenser of justice, the teacher of skills.

You explained the life cycle of the mosquito, the workings of the sewing machine and the orbits of the planets with equal clarity and competence. You

grew cabbages like cannon balls, sweet peas like
butterflies. You showed us how to make a perfect
dove-tailed joint, to make a soufflé, to sew on a
button, to graft a rose. You taught us to look and
listen, to think, to question, to explore.
And then, as if by magic, you turned before our eyes
into a man of ordinary stature - a man who walked
the dog before breakfast and had a little doze after
his Sunday lunch.

You turned into a man rather shorter than
our friends. Courteous, kind, forbearing -
but, as we saw it, rather behind the times.
For we had grown up and found ourselves
other heroes. Or rather, we had half grown up.

Time passed and we grew wiser. And
saw at last that you were truly Superman - who,
once his work for us had been done, chose to
resume his mild disguise.

. . .

BEFORE IT GETS TOO LATE, DAD

Poets are inclined to weep
when their papas are buried deep,
tucked up and out of sight.
They wallow in complete recall,
which doesn't help their dads at all,
or make the wrong things right.
But I'm no poet, so I'll say
all my apologies today
for every teenage fight,
for every laziness and lie,
for every bitterness and sigh
I caused you.... Better live than write,
old love; we'll use our days
in daft, companionable ways
while we've still life and light.

I've always taken you for granted.

Dads, I thought, always knew about stars and seas and far off times and places. They had a great store of anecdotes. They had exactly the right, comfortable voices for reading bedtime books. They taught their children how to whistle. They made them toys. They could tie a fisherman's knot with a flick of the fingers. They could always be relied on to create small adventures. They could mend anything. They were patient and loving and always had a little spare loose change.

Fathers made the whole world safe.

Now I know, of course, I was not just one of the lucky ones.

I was, I am, most singularly blessed.

Dear Dad.

DELAYED THANKS

Dads are ordinary individuals who find themselves responsible for raising another human being to be kind, honest, educated, useful, loving and brave.

All dads deserve a cheer from all their kind, honest, educated, useful, loving, brave children.

. . .

I stand here, an elderly grandmother, and say what I should have said long since. My thanks and my apologies, on behalf of every mother, to all the dads who, while the world revolved around the bed and cradle, vacuumed the house, cleaned the windows,

got in the groceries, notified the newspapers,
sent off the birth announcement, bought a
bear, a welcome-home cake, a copy of the
newspaper, raced to and from the hospital
with shopping lists and clothing, called all
the people who must be told and ferried
them to visit, got indigestion - and was
gently ignored by every nurse in sight. And
whom we forgot to thank.

We were so busy looking at the baby we
never noticed the shining floor and the
dustless living room.

We're sorry. We hope it's not too late to hug
you now - and say we love you.

. . .

THE WORLD NEEDS FATHERS

Here's to the fathers that can turn their hand to anything. Who do the thing that needs doing. Who wipe noses and pull up panties. Who peel the potatoes. Who do the drains. Who whisk and stir and chop. Who have the kids in bed by the time mum gets home from work. Who are there when they're needed.

Who, with mothers, are the hub of the home.

. . .

The world has an infinite need of loving mothers - and finds them everywhere. Quietening the child troubled by bombardment, fighting to save a harvest, making a festival from waste paper and a stub of candle. But they need a companion in the long trek to safety. They need a defender in times of danger. They need someone to share their troubles and to keep hope alive.

The world has an infinite need of loving fathers.

. . .

I reach out my arms to all the fathers of the world,

cut off from their wives and children by war or want

or work... and yearn with the hearts of all those

mothers, all those children, for their return.

Families manage. Families get by.

But that is never enough.

Come home safely.

Come home soon.

. . .

Thank you for guiding me through difficult times. Thank you for standing beside me when I wanted reassurance. Thank you for stepping back and letting me go it alone when the time had come.

THANK YOU FOR EVERYTHING

Thank you for all the stories. Thank you for facing up to Mrs. Thing at school. Thank you for not killing me when I scraped your car.
Thank you for being around.

Thank you for teaching me the value of courtesy and respect by giving them to me, from the time that I was very small.

. . .

Thank you for making me feel that I came first,
whatever the demands on your time and pocket.

Thanks for all the good advice I ignored.
Then.

Thank you for making me understand how unique
and valuable each living thing is - and how each
depends upon the other.

Thank you for making the rules - and bending them
when necessary.

Thank you for teaching me the rewards of silence.

Thank you for convincing me that I am special.
And that I share this gift with every human being.

Thank you for all the mended bikes and glued-
together teddy bears and the cold, wet camping trips
and the dancing demonstrations and ...
Oh, *everything*.

. . .